Passive Income

STEP-BY-STEP HOW TO TURN THE TOP 6 ONLINE STRATEGIES INTO A SINGLE MONEY MAKING MACHINE!

By Jake Whiteley

Copyright © 2016 by Jake Whiteley. All Right Reserved.

No part of this publication may be reproduced, distributed, or transmitted in any form or by any means, including photocopying, recording, or other electronic or mechanical methods, or by any information storage and retrieval system without the prior written permission of the publisher, except in the case of very brief quotations embodied in critical reviews and certain other noncommercial uses permitted by copyright law.

Table of Contents

Chapter 1: Why is Passive Income So Important?

Chapter 2: Kindle Book Publishing

Chapter 3: List-Building

Chapter 4: Affiliate Marketing

Chapter 5: Blog/Website Publishing

Chapter 6: Dropshipping

Chapter 7: Course Creation and Membership Sites

Conclusion

Chapter 1: Why is Passive Income So Important?

You have heard every successful online entrepreneur with his courses; eBooks and blogs passionately advocate passive income. Financial independence is the goal and "Passive Income" is the buzzword for ambitious minds keen on creating alternate and steady sources of online income. So what exactly is financial independence? The ability to have enough financial resources to pay for all your expenses without having to worry about it each month? A buffer expense that allows you to put your time and efforts into a pursuit that may not garner immediate returns? Not having to worry about where your next check will come from to clear utility bills? Well, yes, all this and more. Above all, passive income and financial impendence is about freedom, freedom from investing x amount of time and efforts to get paid for it. It is about getting out of the "bucket carrying" mentality and focus on creating a "pipeline" of wealth.

What do people in jobs essentially do? They put in x amount of hours and efforts to work and get paid in proportion to those hours. As a simple analogy, they carry buckets of income through hard work, and by utilizing their time resources. As long you carry the bucket, the source of income stays active. What happens when you stop carrying the bucket? The income comes to a scary halt. You are left with nothing except some savings.

Passive income is the pipeline that astute income creators install for their wealth creation. It doesn't involve putting in a fixed number of hours to get paid a fixed amount in exchange for those hours. It involves building a solid, dependable and life-time income stream by creating things which add value to people's lives. The time and effort required are limited, and the income potential is virtually unlimited. You build the pipeline just once, and have water flowing through it into your house forever. Get the picture? Little wonder then that passive income is often treated as the holy grail of personal wealth management.

Passive income is all about shifting your focus from financial security to financial freedom. People are often so desirous of the illusion of financial security that jobs bring them (which they are conditioned to believe throughout their formal education period) that they pay a heavy price for it with their freedom. They fail to realize that the cost for their security is often their precious freedom. If you choose security over freedom, you will always be working at the hours and wages dictated by someone else. Hell, even when you eat will be controlled by someone else (lunchtime from 1pm to 2pm only). This is the price most of us pay for security in exchange for true freedom. This is the price we pay for tying our income to a daily grind in place of creating solid sources of ongoing revenue.

Passive income is all about getting the money to roll in even when you are not working, or at least not working at the pace of a traditional job for a stipulated monthly salary. It is about having the freedom to enjoy multiple pursuits in life without having your time tied down by the prospect of using it for income generation.

Above all, passive income is a smart way to leverage your time and efforts to ensure minimal efforts and maximum revenue based on those efforts. It is all about being resourceful and creating multiple income streams to free up your time for doing things you enjoy rather than doing things you are required to do.

Passive income, unlike monthly wage related income, is not related to the actual amount of time spent. It comprises in putting an up-front investment of time and efforts and creating endless pay backs for that effort and time for a very long time. For instance, investing in dividend paying stocks, owning real estate that generates a regular cash flow in the form of rent, writing a book that earns a lifetime of royalties, cutting a musical album, getting royalties for a patented invention or building a steady, income-generating website. You get the gist? Passive income is about creating lifetime income streams that pay you back endlessly or at least for the long haul by putting in limited time or effort or financial resources.

Some people have all the time in the world but no money to enjoy it, while others make all the money in the world without having the time to enjoy it. While the former don't trade their time for money, and invariably land up with no money but lots of time, the latter's money is closely tied to the time invested in generating the money, and hence they are left with no time. Passive income generators have the true freedom to enjoy both – time and money. They have the time to enjoy the money they make and they have the money to engage their free time in enjoyable pursuits.

Why does passive income stack so remarkably well? You have a fixed number of hours a day that are spent on a variety of activities including eating, relaxing, sleeping, indulging in hobbies etc. Your hours ultimately have a pretty fixed cap on the value they have for others, unless of course, you're a celebrity or the CEO of a big company. Even if you have diverse skills, you are able to focus only on a single skill and generate income from it.

On the other hand, let us say, you create a website, book or an investment. Then keep adding to it. Start with one, and then create several. Each revenue generation stream is accompanied by an upfront investment of time or money or efforts or a combination of one or more of these factors. It may require minimal maintenance. When money is tied to time, you can rarely create multiple sources of income. How many income-generating tasks can you really do in a 24-hour period? With passive income, since revenue generation is not tied to time, you have a far greater opportunity to create several revenue streams by trading one-off time, income and efforts to enjoy a lifetime of wealth. Thus, passive income allows you to create multiple income streams.

One of the best parts about creating a virtual passive income stream is that it not just gives you time freedom but also absolute geographical independence. You can literally manage your business from any location ranging from pleasant mountains in summers to chic winter beaches. Unlike conventional wage-earning jobs, you aren't tied down to a single, uninspiring and monotonous location.

That's one of the real values of passive income that several people fail to realize.

Of course, passive income can mostly be harder to generate than a regular salary. It may seem more cumbersome and overwhelming, but you know what they say no guts, no glory. The trade-offs of passive income are way higher. You'll not only enjoy a lifetime of revenue coming in from varied sources but also the time freedom to spend that money. You aren't functioning like a mechanical clock all your life just to fulfill some other visionary's corporate dreams and earn a measly income in exchange your skills.

One of the biggest pluses of building an online passive income stream is that it is fairly inexpensive. You don't have to spend thousands of dollars on purchasing a home and leasing it for income. However, you can start a blog for almost nothing, put in consistent efforts for a while, and it may generate a few hundred a month. Not bad right, with minimal or no investment? It doesn't have the risk of a traditional business (that may need thousands in investment) attached to it, and yet the rewards can be magnificent.

Imagine, you gradually build about 20 sites that bring in an income of 300 dollars each/month. That's 6000 dollars a month long-term income. Good deal? You bet! Though this may seem like an overtly optimistic estimate and not everyone may witness these kinds of results. However, everyone has a fair chance to create these results by investing their time and efforts in educating themselves about creating online passive income sources. It doesn't take a genius or a filthy rich person to start a decent virtual passive income-generating stream. All you need is patience, persistence, and the ability to keep learning/changing and offering people value. So how exactly does a beginner with very little money to invest go about creating powerful online revenue sources? Let us look at my top 6 strategies for creating solid virtual revenue sources that can help you enjoy a lifetime of passive income.

Chapter 2: Kindle Book Publishing

Kindle book publishing is one of the most cost effective, rewarding and realistic online passive income opportunities. It publishes your book on a platform where millions of readers can access it on their Kindle readers, smartphones and tablets. Kindle Direct Publishing and KDP select both offer authors 70 percent royalties for titles priced between $2.99 to 9.99.

Kindle Direct Publishing or KDP Select

The first decision you need to make is choosing between Kindle Direct Publishing and KDP Select. KDP Select has plenty of merits; however, keep in mind that publishing your book on KDP Select requires exclusivity. You can't publish or sell your book on any other platform.

KDP Select lets you offer your book complimentary for the first few days or for a reduced price for a maximum of seven days though the Countdown Deal. You earn 70% royalties throughout the Countdown Deal period. This can help in your book promotion efforts. In addition to this, all KDP Select titles are available on the Kindle Owners' Lending Library, which is a free reading service for Amazon Prime customers. Each time your book is downloaded from the library, you earn a portion of a cumulative monthly fund. They may not give you earth shattering results but these benefits add up considerably to contribute to a decent monthly passive income if you offer value to readers and promote your book well.

If you are just looking to test with limited income initially, restrict to a single publishing platform, which KDP Select offers. Publishing your book everywhere may dilute test results and prevent you from mastering a single platform. Rather than scattering your efforts and time across various platforms, focus your beginner energy on a popular publishing platform like KDP Select for optimal returns. Choosing between Kindle Direct Publishing and KDP Select is a personal decision that authors will have to make depending on their business objectives and nature of online business.

Create a Fantastic Cover

Whether you like it not, a book is judged by its cover. EBooks are no different. An eye-catching, professional and smart-looking cover whets your reader's curiosity and increases the appeal of your book. Remember, it is the only thing Amazon will display to potential readers in the "Customers Who Bought This Item Also Bought" option. You can use a professional graphic designer or outsource to one of the service providers on a digital services marketplace. All you need is a sharp 1563px x 2500 px image. Use vivid colors, well-defined images and bold fonts to create an impressive, attention-grabbing cover.

One of the best tips while designing a cover is to come up with multiple versions and then solicit a preferences feedback from your target audience. It brings to your notice small details you may have otherwise overlooked.

Convert Into A Mobi

While formats such as .doc, PDF, HTML and txt can be uploaded; most Kindle publishing veterans recommend mobi, a format exclusive to Kindle. It might seem like a time-consuming inconvenience but the results are worth it and this is only a one- time conversion effort, which can be used for all future books. Download the free Kindle Previewer and KindleGen. While the former will convert HTML files into the mobi format, the latter gives you an idea of how the book will actually appear on multiple Kindle versions.

The next step is to launch Scrivener, and select the Compile function after locating your book on KindleGen. Just pick the available formatting choices and you are good to go.

Publish

As a thumb rule, upload your book at least 48—72 hours prior to the official launch. This gives you enough buffer time to sort out technical snags and other unforeseen issues. One good tip for publishers looking to gain a breakthrough into the rewarding world of Kindle is to send across a few complimentary copies to family, friends and other associates before the launch. Ask them to leave reviews on the book's Amazon listing. This way you'll feel more confident promoting your book later since you'll already have some great reviews in place for them to reference. Anything between 100-200 free copies should do the trick.

Pick the perfect two categories while uploading your book. This will make all the difference when the bookstore guides potential customers to locate your work while they are actively browsing for topics related to your book, and on the Top 100 list.

Think about potential words and phrases (keywords or key phrases) that your readers are most likely use while finding your book on the Kindle store. What is the fundamental idea behind the book? What does it aim to give the readers? What are the main questions and concerns addressed in the book? Add five to seven keywords or phrases in your product description to help readers find it easily. Next, upload the cover. Hit the "Browse" option and choose your mobi file. Before you click on "Save & Continue", check everything once on Online Previewer.

Next, select you royalty option, which is determined by the book's pricing. You can pick the 70 percent royalty option if the book is priced between $2.99 to $9.99. Unless there's a strong strategy and objective behind it, it doesn't make sense to pick the 35% royalty option and have Amazon enjoy a bulk of your profits.

Reward Early Buyers

Early buyers are most likely royal readers who are already familiar with your blogs or courses or friends on the social media. Reward their loyalty and support in the early stages of your business by offering free copies or discount coupons. You can sell the book at a reduced price for the first few buyers before going back to your original price. In addition to his, incentivize readers to leave genuine reviews in exchange for a discount on your future books or courses. This can generate plenty of reviews.

Another benefit of this strategy is that Amazon quickly picks up titles, which are purchased by several readers at once, and exposes it to even more readers by promoting it. This helps the book bag an impressive rank within a short span.

Promote The Book

For Amazon to help you boost your sales and reach potential readers, its complicated algorithm needs to hit a specific sales volume mark. You will earn the required push from Amazon only when you go about promoting your book first. Spread the word by submitting a few high-quality guest posts that give readers a sneak peak of your expertise to stimulate their curiosity. Create quote memes for interesting lines from the book and share them extensively on social media. Link to your book from your social media updates, guest blog posts and email signature. Plan your promotions well, be creative and keep promoting your book consistently. You get the five Free Days or a Seven-Day Countdown deal with KPD Select which can be resourcefully used for your promotional campaign.

Track Your Results

Use a basic spreadsheet to keep track of your results including your daily sales in different countries. For KDP Select, you also have to take into account the portion earned from a monthly pool every time someone borrows your book. Borrows also determine a book's rank.

Take a periodic overview of reviews left behind by readers. What's the general consensus about the book among readers? What feedback and suggestions can be incorporated into subsequent books? How many reviews have won a five star rating? What are people mostly liking about the book? This can help you stay on track about the book's performance and guide you while drafting future titles.

It is a good idea to track your ranking though some publishers discourage it. Check the sales pages in the Product Details category to check the overall rank of your book in the entire

Kindle Store and subsequently each category. Since rankings are updated each hour, you might get addicted to hitting refresh multiple times during the day. Don't get too overwhelmed by the fluctuating rankings. Just keep promoting your book on multiple platforms consistently. Once your book gains exposure and earns a few good reviews, the rankings will invariably fall into place.

Chapter 3: List-Building

Ask any successful Internet marketer to offer a one-line advice to an online marketing greenhorn and 8 out of 10 will say – build a list. An email list is nothing but a list of email addresses of readers who have subscribed to your newsletter or updates. This list is then used for sending them information about new products, industry related news, offers, freebies and much more. It establishes a direct point of contact for online entrepreneurs looking to connect with potential customers (or subscribers once they subscribe to your newsletters or updates).

The Value of Your List

Contrary to popular perception held by new age online marketers, list building and email marketing is far from dead or replaced by the social media. Ever wondered why you need an email address for signing up for a social media account if that was the case? People still check their mails keenly first thing before getting to the day's work. Email remains one of the most powerful channels of online communication, and building a list ensures you are able to keep in touch with your potential customers regularly, irrespective of changing Google or social media trends.

Email offers a more solid, reliable and dependable marketing channel that's not at the whims of fluctuating algorithms. It frees your dependency of external traffic generation sources. Say for instance, Google changes its algorithms by launching one of its periodic updates. You may end up losing your ranking overnight for reasons that are too complicated to fathom. However, with a quality list, you are not at the mercy of the big G because you already have a ready database of customers who are interested in your products and services. You can wield greater control on your interactions with your target audience and marketing plan, since you are directly connected to your prospective customers.

Take the example of retail giant Amazon. Don't they keep mailing you offers and notify you about sales/discounts continuously? Don't these mails tempt you to have a look and many times lead to buy from them? List building , if done right, can help you enjoy a high conversion rate, a dependable bank of loyal customers and a vast pool of prospective customers actively interested in your products/services.

Lists can bring you repeat sales for your products or repeat traffic for your website/blog. Even if you don't have a physical product, building a list will allow you to quickly get in touch with your customers and inform them about a new blog post or an updated piece of content. The way a list can be used is almost limitless, and can only be restricted by your creativity and resourcefulness. Several successful Internet marketers regard these as the most valuable assets when it comes to building an online business empire. Your money can truly be in your list as it is popularly quoted in Internet marketing circles.

Benefits of List Building

1. Lists help you build a loyal tribe/community of people who trust you, and swear by the

information or products/services offered by you.

2. It is one of the most personal ways to spread the word about your products and services by directly addressing the customer.

3. List building gives you an opportunity to maintain a solid relationship with existing readers or buyers to enjoy repeat sales or blog traffic.

4. You can diversify or experiment with content to what your buyers or readers really like and then fine-tune your products/content to suit their preferences.

5. It is a super brand building initiative. List building allows you to create a clear, focused and strong identity for your brand among potential and existing customers.

6. Mailing lists are generally opt-in options that readers or buyers have voluntarily signed up for. This reduces the chances of your newsletter or update getting thrashed and landing up in spam folders.

7. Lists help you contact you target audience quickly for speedy response marketing campaigns.

8. Email marketing is one of the most cost-effective marketing tools and literally allows you to send marketing messages to a large customer base at the click of a button. Also, since the list is customized to contain email addresses of only those customers who have displayed an interest in your products or information, you have access to a highly focused audience.

9. Advertisers love an exhaustive email marketing list. Sponsors and advertisers will almost always want to know the strength of your mail list. It indicates your loyal customer base, and reinforces your credibility. A strong list will help you negotiate more lucrative advertising deals.

10. The return on investment for well built emailing lists can be huge since we are talking about a laser focused source of traffic. These aren't some random people on the Internet but people who have chosen to stay updated about

your products or services. The only investment is time for creating periodic newsletters and a few software applications to send out mails.

11. Unlike several other marketing and promotional channels, email marketing gives you the opportunity to measure your results accurately. You can check everything from how many subscribers actually opened the mail to how long they read it to details about the links they clicked on.

12. Follow up sales can be a breeze with a thorough and focused mailing list. You don't have to look for new costumers by spending a bomb every time you launch a new product. You already have a ready list of customers who trust your products or services to make repeat purchases from you.

13. Lists allow you convert people who simply display an interest on your products/services into loyal buyers or readers. Thus well-built lists can be formidable conversion channels.

Using eBooks For List Building

Just like every marketing channel, readers will sign up for an email list only when they have a strong incentive to do so. You should be able to answer their "what is in it for me?" to be able to gain their trust and convert them into life-long subscribers.

Offering value in the form of free eBooks is one of the best ways of getting customers to sign up for your periodic updates. The idea is offer such an irresistible value to potential customers that it becomes impossible for them to leave without turning into subscribers.

You can create content by expanding on your already existing blog post or create a handy question and answer book by addressing the most compelling concerns of your target audience related to your topic or offer them a ready to use list – anything that offers immense value and they find hard to turn down. You can update or modify previously published material or draft entirely new content. Try and use the book to address the most pressing questions raised by your readers on social media.

Your final book will be mailed to subscribers in a PDF format, hence limit it to 10 MB. Don't fill it up with several high resolution images that will slow the mailing and downloading process. Design (or get someone to do for you) a professional and attractive looking cover for the book. Keep basic formatting rules in place for a clean, comfortable and visually-appealing layout. Once the book is all done, set up your auto-responder to automatically mail it to be people who enter their details in your list.

Ensure your reader goes through the double opt-in, and that their welcome mail features an attachment or PDF link to the book. Try a variety of professional looking and well-converting sign up forms (that direct them to them to the book) to know what really lures your target audience. You can use preformatted sign up forms which can be easily integrated into your email list. Split test (test with multiple options) your forms so you can tweak colors, designs, visuals, words and call to action accordingly. Test by placing the sign up forms in different places such as end of a blog post or sidebar or beginning of your post. Each form will help you track sign up and impression stats.

You can also sell new books to existing mail subscribers by creating sales launch mails. Another way to market new books is to offer a complimentary copy of your book to all existing customers in exchange for some honest reviews. Send out an attractive newsletter announcing the launch of your brand new book. Let your current subscribers know they are first ones to download it as a special loyalty gift. Also, if the subscribers feel someone will greatly benefit from the book, they can ask them to sign up for your mailing list in exchange for a free copy.

Pro Tips to Keep Your Subscribers Loyal

1. People have subscribed to your list for a specific purpose that holds value for them. Send them content that is useful and benefits them in some way. Keep your updates or newsletters consistent and high on utility. It should be something your users come to

depend on over a period of time. Focus on offering a fundamental type (such as curated content or features or newsletters or giveaways) and build more detailed campaigns based on this core content distribution strategy.

2. Keep the promises you make to your subscribers. If you tell them while opting-in that you'll be sending 20 fresh marketing tips each week or a free 15-day course to their inbox – do it. In fact, go a step ahead and deliver more than what you have promised to win brownie points. People will appreciate when you go beyond the regular (something offered by hundreds of marketers) and throw in more value than others offer.

3. Include a few unexpected deals and surprises to sweeten it up. Everyone loves receiving an occasional and unexpected treat. Your customers are no different. Giving them a discount at a coffee shop or spa is a good way to boost your likability and get customers to stay. Even if they don't use it, it's a warm fuzzy all the way.

4. Keep the right mailing frequency that lurks somewhere between annoying your customers with incessant mails and helping them forget about you. As a rule of thumb (you may modify this based on your marketing objectives and industry), two to three mails a week are decent enough. You will most likely witness a large number of mail list dropouts if you keep bombarding your subscribers with tons of mails each day. Subscribers who stay will get more conditioned to ignore your mails and will not award too much attention even to important updates.

5. Make your messages more personal. People are tired of generic auto-responder mails that sound like they've been drafted by bots. Make your mails stand out by adding a personal touch to it. It can be anything that you think will instantly help you strike a warm rapport with a particular group. Anything current or topical will also grab their interest. For instance if you are in the sports or fitness industry, you can start your mails by referring to the previous night's game. Get chatty and

focus on what drives them to center your mails on it.

6. Keep your mails short, snappy and interesting. These aren't meant to be blog posts or ego massagers. Your subscribers are hit with hundreds of mail broadcasts from different sources. Stand out from the noise by drafting a 300-400 word mail that captures your reader's attention by staying to the point.

7. Reward your loyal subscribers at certain milestones. After consistently sending valuable content to your subscriber's inbox, intersperse your mail updates with surprises that will delight your readers. You can send them appreciation in the form of freebies, discounts or rewards based on certain pre-worked out milestones. This will tell them you really appreciate their continued interest in your services.

8. Do not build random and catch-all lists to target everyone. Use a variety of criteria to segment mailing lists for more effective, laser targeted campaigns. If you have a large content/product/service base, a more targeted

list will be simpler to manage. Break your list into narrower chunks to find more effective ways to create focused campaigns and boost conversions. Customers can complete a small survey at the beginning (mention to the customers that the objective behind this to help serve them better) to give you more in-depth insights into their profile for better segmentation.

Chapter 4: Affiliate Marketing

Affiliate marketing is one of the earliest and most popular methods of creating a steady online passive income stream. It is simply referring someone else's product to your website visitors and earning commissions when people buy the product or perform the required action based on your recommendation links. So every time someone buys a product from your affiliate link or performs an action (such as singing up for a trial of someone else's products), you get a commission on it. The best part about affiliate market is that you are not required to create your own products or services. The effort only boils down to promoting someone else's s goods or services. This doesn't imply that affiliate marketing is a piece of cake. Just like other online income models, it needs time, effort, persistence and constant testing/tweaking to see what works.

The affiliate company gives you a unique tracking URL that helps them track traffic and sales from your website or promotional platform. Several online companies offer an affiliate program on everything from web hosting to footwear. All you need to do is sign up as their affiliate and get the unique tracking link. This link can then be resourcefully inserted into your blog posts for recommending products/services to customers.

For instance, if you are drafting a post related to reviews of the best web hosting services, you can recommend one of the hosts that you are an affiliate for by including the link in your post. Ensure that you stick to recommending only high-quality products/services that have a good standing and credibility. Peddling just about any product just for the sake of a few pennies is not a good strategy if you want to build a dependable and long-term source of income.

13 Power Packed Affiliate Marketing Tips

1 Use a link cloaker if you don't want your affiliate marketing links to look ugly and unprofessional. Cloakers make your link look

short, clean and appealing, which can dramatically improve your click-through rate.

2. Writing reviews is one of the most credible ways to recommend other products and services to people. Pick out the top products/services related to your niche/topic, sign up for their affiliate program and write detailed reviews to promote them. Customers will get the valuable information they are after and you will have a set of potential customers who are already in the buying stage, and are checking out reviews for more insights.

3. Use your email marketing list to promote exceptionally good products and services to loyal subscribers. Remember, the mailing list is your long-term asset. If you keep treating it as a quick money making machine, you'll soon lose subscribers. Promote only those products that you think will benefit your customers or have value for them.

4. Be Honest with your readers. Remember, they always come first. If you notice any glaring shortcomings in the products/services, which you think your readers should know

about, don't be afraid to mention it. This will make you come across as more reliable and credible among potential customers, and they will take your recommendations seriously when you actually pitch good products. Once you lose their trust, they aren't going to be seen anywhere near your website.

5. It will take some money to make money as all businesses. If you want to perform extremely well in affiliate marketing, you will need to invest in a professional looking (not expensive but basic) website that is hosted by a well-known web hosting service along with a catchy domain name that resonates with your target audience. It is also a great practice to personally try out products/services that you recommend for a more trustworthy and authoritative edge. Some companies may not even allow you to sign up for their affiliate program unless you've personally tried their products/services.

4. You might want to start with an affiliate marketing marketplace if you are a newbie. Sites such as Clickbank, Commission Junction, MarketVault, ShareaSale etc. are all

marketplaces for different companies or individuals to list their products/services. You can sign up for these marketplaces, browse through products/services that are relevant to your category and pick products that you would like to promote on your site. These market places are like a one-stop shop that give you access to multiple affiliate marketing programs across different categories.

5. Add bonuses to incentivize customers to buy from you. Make buying from you a value added proposition for customers by throwing in some bonuses or freebies. This works especially well when plenty of competing websites are marketing the same products or services. The bonus can be anything from a report about how to use the product or optimize the value of a service to free Ebooks related to the topic of the products/services you are promoting. For instance, if you are running a wedding related blog and are an affiliate marketer for a company that sells wedding bands, you could throw in a free eBook about the best tropical honeymoon destinations or something similarly related to your target audience (in

your case soon to be married couples) for customers who purchase through your referral link.

6. Ensure you understand the legal fine print. As an affiliate marketer, you should go through the terms and conditions of an affiliate program in detail to understand and comply with them for avoiding legal violations. Adhere to all the legal terms, and aim to do your business in an honest and ethical manner. If you are focusing on affiliate marketing as a long term revenue generation method, focus on creating high quality websites that offer readers valuable content and credible product recommendations.

7. There's no right time to start monetizing your blog. One of the most common bloopers newbie bloggers make is to wait for a while before they start monetizing their blog. As long as you have a few posts on your website/blog before you hit launch, there really is no good time to begin earning revenue from it. There's always something you can sell and promote related to your niche. You can even go about signing up as an affiliate for your webhosting,

domain name or premium theme company by writing a few posts about how readers can create a similar website if they wish to with the help of tools you are personally using. Start as soon as possible, and keep adding to your content database by creating high-quality, well-researched, exhaustive and interesting content that adds value to your readers' lives.

8. Promote products that your readers are most likely to purchase. For instance, if you are running a budget travel blog, you aren't going to witness much success with promoting luxury concierge services or customized holiday packages. Match your products/services with the overall tone of your blog, and the buying patterns of your target visitors.

9. Diversification is the key. Refrain from banking on a single product or service to generate your affiliate marketing commissions. Diversify and promote multiple products belonging to your website/blog topic. For instance, if you run a wedding planning related blog, you can run affiliate marketing

promotions for everything from honeymoon packages to bridal jewelry to trousseau.

10. Make your images clickable too. Other than the links, ensure that the photographs of products and services you're promoting also lead to the sales page. It is frustrating for the customer to enthusiastically click on an image only to be led to an ugly looking image upload page. In the era of visual marketing websites such Pinterest, it can be a huge mistake to not make your images clickable.

11. Get resourceful and become the affiliate marketer for brick and mortar businesses as well. While several newbies are jostling for space in an overcrowded universe of online affiliate markets, be slightly different and try to utilize the channel of traditional businesses for generating your affiliate commissions. For instance, if you run a home improvement blog, you can earn a neat commission from contractors in your area by capturing local potential customer leads for them or if you run a New York City blog that lists the most happening events, activities and trends for locals, you can capture details of potential

customers wanting to sell or buy property in NYC and sell the leads to local real estate brokers on a per lead commission basis.

12. Always be transparent with your readers by disclosing affiliations upfront. A full disclosure of the fact that you will be making a commission by promoting certain goods/services will be appreciated by customers. You will come across as honest and ethical in your approach, which is so vital if you are looking to build a long term passive income channel. It is also a legal binding to include a full disclaimer of your affiliations while recommending products/services. You can offer customers incentives such as discounts, bonuses and freebies, but always make sure they know you are doing it for a referral credit.

13. Keep testing different ads to measure what works. The most successful online passive income earners are the ones who keep testing and adapting according to user behavior. Spend some time thinking about your users' typical browsing patterns. Where are they most likely to spot particular ads? Can you

blend text ads seamlessly within the content to make recommendations appear more natural? Try rotating multiple graphic and text based ads before identifying the ones that yield maximum result. Though this is not a thumb rule, digital products (with their higher commissions) may be more lucrative than regular products.

Chapter 5: Blog/Website Publishing

Once your click the "Publish" button, your blog post is out there for the world to see forever. You can write a valuable blog post about a topic concerning your target audience today, and have them reading and benefiting from it years from now. Thus, the blog becomes a steady source of income for you even 5-6 years after you've originally published the post. Each post gives you the chance of connecting with your customers, strengthening your relationship with them by offering value, reinforcing your authority in a niche and gaining a loyal reader base that trust you.

Blogs are also a great channel for boosting other sources of income described in the book, such as giving readers more information about your eBook topics or offering a unique membership course. Blogs convey the human side of your business by establishing a strong connect with the audience before actually selling to them. They make you come across as someone who cares for your reader's welfare enough to offer them solid value propositions than simply selling to them like a hungry marketer.

Once you have a well-researched, professionally written, SEO (Search Engine Optimization) synchronized and easily navigable blog that earns a steady stream of traffic, it is easy to monetize it using one of the several ways, including affiliate marketing, signing up for advertising programs such as Google Adsense, selling eBooks, selling leads to local businesses, offering email courses, setting up Banner Ads, offering services for other businesses, selling your own products and much more. Here's an easy to follow guide for setting up your own profitable blog.

Decide on a topic

Pick a blog topic that you are passionate and fairly knowledge about, as it will invariably reflect in your writing. Don't simply go with topics that are popular among bloggers. Pick one where you are confident about creating authoritative and unique content. Tap into your educational background, hobbies, pervious jobs etc to know where your expertise lies and then share those experiences with readers.

Do not keep your blog niche/topic too broad. Look for unique angles or sub-niches to make it more focused and in-depth about a specific sub-topic. Broad topics will not help you cover very specific topics intensively and you'll end up facing too much competition from the big fishes. Aim to be a big fish in a small pond rather a small fish in the ocean. For instance, instead of simply having a travel blog that gives people information about different places, how about a blog focusing on Caribbean luxury travel? Or rather than simply having a blog about diet recipes (which a hundred other blogs are covering), how about diet breakfast recipes? You get the gist, right? Come up with new and unique angles to make your content more focused and searchable.

Select the Right Blogging Platform

While there are several free blogging platforms out there, if you are serious about turning your blogs into sources of passive income, you should ideally go with a WordPress self-hosted option. WordPress is one of the most beginner-friendly versatile and visually-appealing platforms for creating blogs/websites. You have the choice of picking your blog's domain name and web hosting service if you are self-hosting the blog. Unlike the free WordPress option, the self-hosted one gives you the flexibility of setting up banner ads and inserting affiliate marketing links. A free WordPress blog will appear like this – mylowfatcooking.wordpress.com, while the URL for your self-hosted blog will be – mylowfatcooking.com. The latter looks professional, and has tons of features to beautify and simplify your blogging activities.

Domain Name and Web Hosting

Opt for a catchy, brandable and unique domain name that defines your blog's personality from a domain name registrar such as GoDaddy or Namecheap. Keep it short, relevant and easy to remember. Avoid names of brands or famous personalities as you may get on the wrong of the law due to copyright issues. Avoid opting for domain names with characters. Doesn't my-low-fat-cooking.com or my.low.fat.cooking.com kill the appeal of your URL? Besides a domain name without characters is easier to remember and access.

Use appropriate domain name extensions. The most popular option still remains .com as customers always relate to a site as .com. The next best if a .com is not available is to go with a .net or .org. Ensure the extension goes with the overall tone of your blog. You do not want a .club extension when you are running a blog that hasn't got anything remotely related to a club. Opt for the Privacy Protection option offered by domain registration companies (some offer it free for the first year, otherwise comes for around $9.99/year) if you wish to protect your personal details from appearing in a public website ownership database.

There are plenty of web hosting companies such as Hostgator and BlueHost that can offer you hosting services if you opt for a self-hosted blog. Start with a basic and work your way up once you have a steady stream of visitors. Look for coupons that give you hosting services free for a month or at a reduced price ($3-

5/month). Since most hosting companies offer a 30-day money back guarantee, you do not have to worry about being committed to a single company.

Check out several online reviews for hosting companies and go with a web host that has a favorable uptime, impressive customer/technical support service and solid security. There are many companies that'll throw in some freebie such as complimentary business email accounts. You may opt for these but do not compromise on basic features such as security and technical support.

Designing Your Blog

Choose a free WordPress theme or purchase a premium theme from services such as Themeforest. net. Free themes work fine for newbies, however you can opt for premium themes if you want to add more frills to the blog. Go to the Appearances-Themes section and pick a theme that resonates with the overall feel of the blog. WordPress allows you to change themes instantly by hitting a few buttons.

Increase your blog's stickiness (in Internet marketing jargon, the ability of a blog to keep its customers hooked) by keeping the interface visually appealing, easy to navigate and well-organized. If you make it tough for attention-deprived customers to find information they are looking for, they'll jump to the next easily navigable blog. Make navigation a cakewalk for readers by segregating your blog posts into appropriate categories, balancing text with enough white space and using an easy on the eye color combination. Get a graphic artist to design a nice looking and unique header for the blog.

Make your blog posts more readable for users who wish to quickly scan through the content. Use lots of subheads, tables, infographics, quotes and bullets to help important bits of text stand out. Keep paragraphs short and title them correctly. Create sidebar text in a larger font to make it more noticeable. Color contrasts should be judiciously used. These are some vital pointers to boost your blog's readability. Ensure you pick a blog theme that is responsive i.e. it identifies different devices such as tabs and smartphones and optimizes the appearance of the blog on the particular device by resizing pictures, altering the navigation bar, changing the side widgets and more.

10 Brilliant Ways to Monetize Your Blog

1. Sign up for a popular ad program such as Google Adsense. You are basically doing nothing but "renting" space to Google for them to display their advertiser's ads on your blog. Google keeps the advertisements related to your content. Each time a blog visitor clicks on the ad, you earn a small commission. Once you have a collection of published posts and consistent traffic, you can continue to earn from Adsense for years.

2. When you have a dependable source of traffic, start directly selling banner advertising space to companies related to your blog topic. For instance, you may want to approach travel companies and airlines if you run a travel related blog. You eliminate the middlemen and can charge any amount you deem fit. Your advertisers will be more than willing to pay

you if you can drive business their way consistently.

3. Affiliate marketing as we've already discussed above is an easy and rewarding way to make money by marketing other people's goods or services. Pick high quality and relevant products/services that will add value to your audience's life. Write well-researched, detailed and compelling reviews around these products and help your customers buy rather than just selling to them.

4. Sell digital products such as eBooks or email courses. Information reports and eBooks have gained immense popularity in the last few years due to e-readers and other reader-friendly applications. Create a comprehensive and thoroughly researched eBook about any aspect that you think profoundly affects your target audience or something they have a deep interest in. This can be sold directly from your blog by informing subscribers about it through a newsletter. Another alternative is to put it up for sale on Amazon with a link directed to your blog in the author bio field.

People who are impressed with the book will come back to the blog for more. And subscribers who swear by the valuable content on your blog will be tempted to purchase the book. It is all about being resourceful and creating a symbiotic relation between different platforms to maximize your passive income.

5. Hosting a webinar. Webminars are primarily real time workshops where people pay to watch presentations and/or demonstrations made by experts. You may need to gather a considerable subscriber base before utilizing this monetization method, though it can be extremely lucrative once established. Conduct live workshops on anything from how to build a WordPress Blog to DIY woodwork. You can include everything from power point slides to images to opinion polls etc to make your presentations more interactive and impressive. Questions can be addressed at the end of the webinar. The best part is people from all over the planet can participate in your webinar.

6. Paid membership sites are another great monetization method. For a fixed monthly or annual fee, you can offer your readers lots of

valuable tools, resources and information related to your industry. For instance if you run a design related blog, you can offer paid members downloadable animation models or step-by-step tutorials on creating the perfect object designs. You need to offer lots of unique and valuable resources that your users cannot find in many other places to keep them hooked or they'll eventually fade out and look for free services elsewhere.

7. Paid directory listings are another great way to leverage the popularity of your blog. You can reserve a specific space on your blog for listings of products/services related to your blog topic. For instance, if you run a blog about writing digital media copy and have a steady audience flow comprising web writers and bloggers, you can start a paid directory listings service for business or websites looking for digital content writers. The companies will end up finding good writers who are keen on enhancing their skills, the writers will get rewarding assignments and you will get a fee for listing the post.

8. Sell your own templates. If you have created a unique and customized theme, consider selling it through your blog. Several blog owners are shopping around for unique themes and your theme might be exactly what they are looking for. This can become another easy source of regular income from your blog.

9. Get into a pay per lead arrangement with local businesses. If you have a location or local business specific blog, consider getting into a business arrangement with local businesses for paying you per lead you generate for them. For instance, if you run a blog related to Antigua Islands located in the Caribbean, you can tie up with local real estate brokers for paying you per vacation home buying prospect lead you send their way.

10. Write paid reviews and promotional posts for companies. If you have a considerable reputation or are seen as influencer in your industry, you can get paid to write reviews and promote products/services related to your blog niche. For instance, many popular mommy bloggers get paid to write posts promoting

child care products to their target audience. Companies benefit because they get access to a ready group of interested buyers who trust the opinion of the blogger. However, ensure you maintain a good balance with non-promotional content or you will lose credibility by coming across as too "salesy" for your readers. If you have used a product and benefitted greatly from it, go ahead and promote it to your readers to make their lives easier.

Chapter 6: Dropshipping

Dropshipping is one of the most convenient, rewarding and easy to begin passive income opportunities for newbies. In simple words, it is about using wholesalers (who offer dropshipping services) to get them to directly ship products to your customers. You take orders via your ecommerce platform and forward them to the dropshipping company. The wholesaler dropshipping company then fulfils your order by dispatching the product to your customer for you.

There is no hassle of maintaining and stocking a product inventory. Also, there is no hassle about losing money on unsold products because you get paid before your product is dispatched to the customer. You can sell a large variety of products without worrying about warehouse and storage related expenses. It is precisely for this reason that dropshipping has become one of the most profitable home business models. Find a credible dropshipper who features products you wish to retail. Get a bunch of appealing product images from the dropshipping firm and display it on your website. When the customer hits on the buy button, you place an order with the dropshipping company, who in turn ships the product to your customer.

10 Tips for Picking A Great Dropshipping Product Niche

Profit Per Sale – Pick a niche that has products offering you a decent gross profit per sale. If you make a meager $10-20 per sale, it will be hard for you to cover business costs. Choose products that can be sold for $300 or more as a general rule to be able to make enough profits to cover your expenses. Average drop-shipping profit margins are about 20% - 25%, so if your product value is $400, you'll end up with a gross profit of $80 per product. The greater your order value, the higher your profits. Most people who make a killing with dropshipping sell items priced $1000 and above.

However, keep in mind that higher product costs also translate into greater service expectations. Your customers will expect better services in terms of direct telephonic contact or technical assistance or pre-sales information. You must have the infrastructure to fulfill services. Keep profit margins large enough to rationalize these support related expenses.

Unique Products – Opt for products that are not easily available to your target audience locally. Anything that customers have a trouble sourcing from the local market is searched online. Your store will be all set and waiting to handle an influx of orders if you sell products that are not widely found in local markets.

Strength and Influence of Competitors – A majority of general drop shopping companies have too many players to help you earn a decent share of the overall profit pie. The trick is to find a really unusual niche and dominate it by being one of the first players in that niche. If any niche has about 4-5 solid and established companies, give it a miss. You may also come across just 1-2 competitors but they may be really big players who have been around for ages, and have a large and happy customer base. Again, you may not stand a good chance of beating their credibility and customer loyalty. On the other hand, you may find a niche that has zero competitors. This can be either because the product doesn't have a large enough market or you've come across a solid untapped niche. If it is the former, you will have to abandon the niche, but if it is the latter, you may want to consider it. There's no set rule – you just have to research and investigate further to know if your niche has enough demand to make substantial profits.

Can You Add Value to The Niche – With every average Joe jumping on the ecommerce bandwagon, do you have some special skills that can add value to your customers? Do you have passion or at least a fair knowledge about the niche? If you are selling worldwide postage stamps for philately enthusiasts, are you able to establish a brief and interesting context/history for these stamps? Or if you are selling home décor items, are you knowledgeable and creative enough to offer your patrons valuable home decoration tips? This value addition can make a huge difference in your profits. You customers can purchase these products from other sources as well, but if you offer additional value in terms of knowledge, tips and ideas, they will view you as a credible seller within your niche.

Speculate Future Trends – After you have determined a favorable price point and low competition, speculate future trends related to your products. Do you reckon people will tend to spend more on your niche in future because the market is only slated to grow? Do you see a remarkable growth for camping related activities in future that you can cater to with a more exhaustive range of camping products? Are people more likely to spend time indoors or outdoors in future? Is there any powerful and growing trend that you can cash on in the coming years (think gadget accessories)? You get the flow right? Gauge the demand for your niche in the coming years to make it a powerful source of long-term income.

Seasonality of the Product – Opt for a product that can be profitably sold throughout the year by following a usual sales cycle. A typical sales cycle sees an increased demand for products from September to peak in

November – December. The cycle then slows down considerably between January to March to rise in April to June. There is a slump in July and August. Now, if you are selling snowboarding gear, your sales period may last only during winters from October to February. You will be struggling to stay afloat through the rest of the seasons. Stay away from product niches that are affected by weather or other frequently fluctuating conditions and opt for those that can be purchased throughout the year.

Repeat Purchases – Another vital niche selection factor should be repeat purchases. Do customers come back to purchase the product? Or is it just a once in a lifetime kind of buy? As any savvy entrepreneur will tell you, it is easier and cheaper to retain/sell to old customers than acquiring new buyers. Having repeat customers gives you the leverage to grow exponentially without spending a fortune on acquisition costs. Unless you have a huge target audience in a booming market, you need repeat purchases to witness exponential business growth. The ideal is of course to find a product niche that has a sizeable purchase price and that people often purchase.

Shipping and Return Issues - Take into consideration the size of the product to pick product niches that do not require special delivery or those that witness more than normal returns. You may want to avoid items that need special delivery or absurd shipping expenses. If you want to operate in a niche that incurs huge deliver related expenses, research what your competitors are doing. Are they making customers pay for shipping or hiking prices and offering free shipping? If you are unable to bear the heavy shipping expenses, you are better off picking another niche.

Also, check how often products in your category get returned. You want to minimize these returns to run a hassle free and profitable drop-shipping business. You may want to read actual buyer reviews to gauge the quality and user satisfaction quotient. Keep away from product niches that have multiple variants such as colors, size, type etc. These are more likely to witness return /replacement demands than universal products.

Use Products That Go With Your Existing Blog – Dropshipping can be a wonderful monetization method for an already existing blog. You can sell products related to your blog niche to an already hungry and enthusiastic audience. For instance, if you have a large number of subscribers following your fishing blog, you can sign up with a fishing and angling equipment dropshipper to offer your blog audience the opportunity to conveniently buy fishing gear at the click of a button. Similarly, for a wedding planning tips related blog, selling unique wedding favors can be a great idea. You already have a ready base of subscribers who trust you and have a keen interest in your niche. Selling to these customers is easier than acquiring new customers in a different product niche.

Well Defined Targeted Audience – It is easier to sell when you know exactly who your target audience is. For instance, sports equipment is so vast that you don't have a well-defined enough audience to target them specifically. What game are you focusing on? Are you catering to newbies or professional athletes? Dabbling in a vast niche will make it tough for you to target specific groups. Rather, opting for archery equipment for beginners may give you a more laser targeted audience.

Shopify For Building Easy Ecommerce Sites

1. Sign up for a Shopify account (they have a 14-day free trial for you to test) by entering your details and hit the "Create Your Store Now" button. You need to create a unique store name.

2. You will be asked to provide additional details such as name, physical address and a telephone number. If you are just trying out the service, choose "I am just playing around" and "I am not sure" under the "Do you have products?" option. Finally, click I am done once you have entered all details.

3. Next, head to your store's admin screen and start customizing the store's appearance and features, including setting up shipping and payment related options.

4. Pick a theme that best suits the nature of your products. You can opt for free or premium themes (that feature several modification options). Themes can be sorted by industry, popularity and other features. Check out reviews by existing users and ensure the theme you choose is responsive. View the theme demo and hit "Publish as my Shop's Theme" if you are happy with the overall appearance and layout of your store. You can easily change the theme later if you want to tweak your store look. Go to the Admin-Themes section of your store to make changes to the theme.

5. For adding products select the "Products" option at the left side of the screen. Later, hit the "Add a Product" button located at the top of the web page. Use the next screen to add as many details about your products as possible. Add SEO details including name of the product and a few description lines to make it easier for your customers to find your products while searching for it online. Include all the variants such as colors etc. on your descriptions page.

6. Set up collections for making it easier for customers to access specific products. For instance, clothes designed specifically for newborns or specific types of items such as lamps or carpets or living room accessories. Items can also be categorized into collections based on sizes and colors. Collections are generally displayed on the homepage navigation bar to make it easier for customers to search for what they want rather than rummaging through the entire catalogue.

7. Choose the right payment gateway depending on the features, price and commissions. Keep in mind factors such as transaction features, card types accepted by your gateway and offsite checkout features offered by the payment gateway.

8. You may lose out on a considerable number of sales if your shipping prices are restrictive or you do not offer sufficient shipping choices. Shopify calculates shipping rates based on the details defined by you in the Admin – Shipping page. To make any changes, simply go there and choose a weight determined shipping fee.

The fee should be adjusted according to your merchandise's unique specifications.

Chapter 7: Course Creation and Membership Sites

Using all the methods described above, you can create highly profitable membership sites that can become evergreen sources of passive income. One of the most important features of a membership site or course is to offer prodigious value to your customers. You have to go beyond what the usual free sites offer to keep paid customers on the list for years.

If you are already earning a decent monthly income from a group of loyal customers, it is a good idea to create power-packed, in-depth and useful content that helps them live a successful, rewarding and fulfilling life. The way it works is – your business/blog will have a separate membership site that will offer exclusive content only for members who pay you a fixed monthly fee.

Here are some of the best pro tips for running a successful membership site that becomes a solid source of passive income for you.

Research Membership Sites/Courses You Follow

If you are looking to replicate the success of a particular membership site/course you follow, study their practices diligently and take action. You may already be subscribed to a bunch of sites in your area of interest to gain more knowledge or resources from them. What is it they do differently? It the website navigation-friendly? How many blogs/articles/videos do they add per week? What unique personality and value addition have they created to beat competitors? How have they developed a strong sense of community? Do they have an active discussion forum?

Look at membership sites that don't fare well. What are they doing to mar their chances of creating a popular membership site? What can they do to enhance the user experience? All these aspects will help you develop a blueprint for a well-received and valuable membership site. Concentrate on fundamental aspects as well as smaller details to know what really works.

Give Away a Few Free Spots

You can give out a few free spots to your most active or loyal mailing subscribers. Some may love to hop aboard but may not be able to afford the fees. If they are the folks who are always leaving insightful and valuable comments that help others or are committed readers of your site, get these pleasant folks in. They are most likely your most avid readers and can add tremendous value to the site. You can also consider getting them aboard on a discounted price if a freebie appears too profit margin eating.

Another pro tip is to give away a few copies to influencers in your industry who can spread a good word about your products/services. User-generated marketing can boost your organic promotion efforts like few others. These influencers can reach a wider audience by writing reviews and recommending your products/services. Make it clear to them that they should review your site objectively and are free to bring out its flaws, if any. Users are smart enough to recognize impartial reviews from blatant plants.

Use Platforms You Already Own

Let us assume by now you already have a decent blog and mailing list that brings in steady income each month. Membership site or course creation is the next logical step to build an evergreen source of passive income. You do not have to build a brand new blog in an altogether different niche if you have been active in a particular niche for some time now. Just build your membership site on the existing niche, where you have a ready bunch of loyal followers eager to buy from you. Membership sites are not so much about acquiring a new audience as about catering to an already existing group of loyalists. All you need to do is add a few membership site plug-ins (Membership 2 or Paid Memberships Pro) on your existing WordPress blog and you are good to go.

Build Strong Customer Relationships

An insightful RightNow survey says that 73% of customers vote for good customer service as the single attribute that makes a business endearing to them. Create a passionate community of customers by building strong relationships. Interact with your customers regularly on the social media, create a forum for addressing beginner queries, provide quick email resolution, respond to criticism as gracefully as praise and always solicit valuable feedback about improving your services.

Ask your members for their most pressing concerns or questions before you go about creating a new course or adding content to your site. This will help you give them exactly what they want, thus increasing the likeability and trust even further.

Create fuzzy introductory videos/webminars to highlight the human angle of your sites and make new members feel special. Conduct regular polls to gauge the overall user sentiment. Keep the buzz alive by triggering interesting, informative and topical discussions.

Do Not Delay Until You Achieve Perfection

One of the biggest roadblocks for most passive income creators is their propensity to wait for the "right time". The right time is now. Stop trying to achieve perfection and just start once you have a reasonably established following. You can start with pre-launch or early bird offers to gauge the general sentiment of the course or site. The biggest and brightest success stories belong to those who take action, not the ones who simply read about doing things and wait until eternity to strike.

Your membership site will always be a "work-in-progress" that may constantly be tweaked and modified based on feedback from existing customers and new member requests. This doesn't mean you should just lie low and fill your site with garbage. Build solid content, offer value to customers, generate revenue and build an impressive momentum as you go along.

Engage Users With Podcasts

Move over Facebook and Twitter, Podcasting is the hottest discussion topic among Internet marketers. It is similar to on-demand radio or video. Podcasts are nothing but audio or video files that can be downloaded on enabled devices and consumed on the move. Millions of people love to utilize their time productively while driving, working out or just relaxing at home. Create an engaging, insightful and educational podcast to offer your valuable members "content on the move" under a powerful podcast brand.

Apart from sharing valuable content, your podcasts are also promoting your brand's personality. Pack punch in your audios or videos by making them fun (you can add an element of wit into any niche), personal, less monotonous and attention-grabbing. Your content flow, user engagement and overall personality will influence the podcast audience experience. Invest in quality recording equipment such as microphones/video recorders, recording and editing apps, tools for uploading your files on the web and more.

Podcasts will make your content more entertaining, varied and interactive. You will give your busy members more options for accessing content to keep them onboard.

Create a Power-Packed Webinar

Technology-enabled tutorials and guides are gaining immense popularity due to its versatility and flexibility. Webinars are real time or recorded videos that allow a large bunch of users spread across the world to learn from a single or group of presentations.

Make your webinars smashing by adding lots of interactivity in terms of polls, discussions and questions. This increases user participation and keeps your audience excited right until the end. Invite ideas, concepts and suggestions at the end of every session.

Graphics are the backbone of your webinars. Use them generously and trim down the text matter to make trainings more digestible. Get creative with graphics while explaining certain ideas and concepts. Time your audio piece precisely according to animations, videos and transitions that are a part of your webinar presentation.

Create a blueprint first to determine the flow of your presentation. You will be addressing a global audience. Hence, keep colloquial terms and cultural references at bay, and use more universal concepts.

About the Author

Jake Whitley has been actively involved with SEO and Internet marketing since 2008. Before taking the necessary steps to create his own online business' Jake spent four years working as a SEO consultant and specialist at one of the UK's leading search engine optimization agencies. Since branching out on his own he has become well known in his community for brand building and product creation. His passion has become creating truly passive streams of income by utilizing the latest techniques and social media.

Conclusion

Thank you once again for downloading this book.

I hope it was able to help you to understand the simplest, cheapest and most power-packed ways to create steady streams of passive income online.

The next step is to get up and get going.

You need to take action to create wonderful things and not just keep reading about them until you think you are perfect. Just start and you will invariably achieve perfection along the way.

Use all the action-oriented, practical and step by step strategies mentioned in the book to create solid and dependable sources of income that will award you both financial and time freedom to do everything you have always wanted to do in your life!

Finally, if you enjoyed reading this book, take time to share your insights and thoughts by positing a review. I'd very much appreciate it.

www.ingramcontent.com/pod-product-compliance
Lightning Source LLC
Chambersburg PA
CBHW060412190526
45169CB00002B/870